A DECADE

OF

NEGRO SELF-EXPRESSION

Compiled by

ALAIN LOCKE

Professor of Philosophy, Howard University, Washington, D. C.

With a Foreword by

HOWARD W. ODUM

Director of the School of Public Welfare, University of North Carolina

ISBN: 978-1-63923-789-0

Printed: March 2023

Published and Distributed By:
Lushena Books
607 Country Club Drive, Unit E
Bensenville, IL 60106
www.lushenabks.com

ISBN: 978-1-63923-789-0

Foreword

The untouched picture of the American Negro's cultural development during the decade immediately following the Great War has nowhere, so far as I know, been presented so directly and effectively as in the story of self-expression revealed in the major writings of contemporary Negro authors. And the story is convincing and satisfying. It is vivid, factual and objective. It has the advantage of being artistic and it does not confuse or identify racial traits with cultural forms. Presentation in this form also eliminates the common liabilities found in the human factors of prejudice, limited observation, and inadequate knowledge.

The turn of a century, the rise of an epoch, the aftermath of a conflict, the stirrings of a social process—these are always of importance in their elemental significance to people and nation. This is particularly true of the Negro. In no aspect of the American scene has recent transformation been more marked or development more accelerated perhaps than that in which the intellectual Negro has played his part. To say that it is an unusual record is commonplace. Professor Robert E. Park has referred to this renaissance as a new philosophy of life, a rational basis of new hopes, new attitudes and new racial and social traits. It is important, therefore, he thinks, to judge Negro literature as an "integral part of a single tradition, and as a unique collective experience."

Dr. Locke, in the present paper, has well referred to the new expression as a sort of composite picture of the new Negro mind and spirit reflecting its influence upon Negro life. It is, of course, not entirely new. It is a development, a summation. It is old and it is new. It is exceptional and it is also representative as may well be seen from the remarkably large number of younger Negroes who have felt the creative urge. From every state, in every walk of life they have tried. They have failed and they have succeeded. The record presented in this *Occasional Paper* which Dr. Dillard offers among the publications of the Slater Fund is one index of the measured successes.

Interpretative comment in this foreword would scarcely be in harmony with the form and spirit of the paper. One may, however, look at the picture and report some of the things which he thinks he sees there. Literary portraits reflecting a new realism. A new frankness and courage to face facts without fear, excitement, or apologies. Pride and artistry in the rediscovery and interpretation of a rich folk-background of the race. Acclaim of youthful authors, valued and valuable, but not infallible or supremely mature. A remarkable quantitative achievement, yet expecting a qualitative sequel. A new understanding of the challenge to achieve universal, as well as racial, standards of, excellence. Race consciousness and urge alongside integral participation in American life and cultural development. A race and a national epoch. The promise of balance and poise in an over-enthusiastic and highly charged atmosphere. A new tolerance, charity, and patience. A mellowed bitterness. A mature vision of racial co-operation, race development and understanding. A new outlook and with it a new zest, well tempered by the twin forces of opportunity and obligation.

HOWARD W. ODUM.

Chapel Hill, N. C.
June 1, 1928.

A Decade of Negro Self Expression

BY ALAIN LOCKE,

Howard University

This pamphlet is little more than an annotated list of books written by Negroes since the outbreak of the World War. With it as a guide, however, the modern minded reader may launch out on his own quest for the new facts and points of view in the field of Negro life and experience, with the definite expectation, if he persists, of making his improved knowledge of the Negro part of that new understanding of the world and of human nature which today the changing social order demands of us all. During this period the Negro mind and spirit have been revolutionized; no province of human life has been subject to greater change, few as great. Here in this new body of cultural self-expression is the portrait of the changed and changing Negro. What we today call the "new Negro" is just the composite picture of this new mind and spirit reflecting its influences upon Negro life.

How distinctive, how new and promising this new spiritual world which the Negro mind is creating and into which it is passing, many will never know. For many minds still halt at the wall of prejudice. It is noteworthy and fortunate that the Negro spirit, once in the same predicament with respect to itself and an outlook on life, has found a door, and passed beyond blind controversy to lucid understanding. A young Negro poet puts it—

> We are not come to wage a strife
> Of swords upon this hill,
> It is not wise to waste our life
> Against the stubborn will;
> But we would die, as some have done,
> Beating a way for the rising sun.

Modern America, we think and hope, will leap the self-imposed barriers; will find or make an open door through which it may pass to a voyage of social exploration and discovery. And if so, there will not only come as a result of the venture more light on the Negro, but a new vision and practical faith in democracy.

No one rightly aware of the changes in Negro life would put trust today in indirect information or casual observation as his means of knowing the Negro. There is only one way to this now, and that is the direct approach, the immediate first-hand study of Negro self-expression and cultural self-revelation. More material has been produced in the last decade than in two or three preceding generations. Negro literature has grown by leaps and bounds, and its outstanding exponents are, apart from their racial influence and significance, in many instances figures and factors in general American culture. One result of this is a revolutionized conception of the Negro, by others as well as himself, considered in the role not of an imitator and assimilator of American civilization merely, but of an active contributor to it. In contrast with "the old immemorial stereotype"—to use James Weldon Johnson's words— "that the Negro in America is nothing more than a beggar at the gate of the nation, waiting to be thrown the crumbs of civilization, that he is here only to receive; to be shaped into something new and unquestionably better" comes this new "awakening to the truth that the Negro is an active and important force in American life; that he is a creator as well as a creature; that he has given as well as received, and that he is the potential giver of larger and richer contributions."

This will be the first of an open-minded reader's conclusions. His second will be the realization that the advance elements of Negro life today, instead of being regarded as entirely "exceptional," are felt, by the Negro at least, and increasingly by intelligent observers generally, to be "representative." Genius is always the elite, but Negro genius is nowadays no more exceptional than the genius of other peoples with a functioning sense of group tradition and common destiny. Though far in advance of the multitude, it acts consciously as their advance-guard. Its attainments bring direct pride and inspiration to the rank and file, who with the newly acquired sense of solidarity share and participate in the recognition and general enlightenment which come in ever increasing measure. Much more important than the present achievement is the quickening and releasing influence it will undoubtedly exert for the future. And so we may speak more legitimately than ever of the endeavor and achievement of individuals as Negro effort and Negro progress.

One important thing will instantly be noticed by the keen observer. That is a general desire in this forward thrust toward cultural expression and achievement, not to be patterned entirely by the general drift and trend of colorless conformity to American life, a desire not to be merely imitative. A half generation back, assimilation was the prevailing idea in Negro endeavor. Now it seems pointed in the direction of distinctive achievement; a capitalization of the race's endowments and particular inheritances of temperament and experience. However this movement is not separatist in a limiting sense; it is no voluntary counterpart to the segregation reaction of an intolerant dominant majority. Rather is it a minority promotion move—an attempt to capitalize and bring one's own stock to par, and to have a quotable market rating and a recognized market standing.

An occasional book or two written before 1914 has been included in the list, like Booker T. Washington's "Up from Slavery" or "Souls of Black Folk" by Doctor Du Bois, because within this period in which we are interested they have established themselves as Negro classics and come into the prime of their influence. But ninety per cent or more of the list is of quite recent date, registering in fact the reoriented views of the last few years and our younger generation, who have in general turned from propaganda to art, from cultural parade to self-expression, and in the field of social discussion from controversy and apologetics to scientific social analysis and constructive social criticism.

With these few compass points of direction in hand, the reader may make his own excursion in this venture of human exploration and understanding. He can keep a true and progressive course through no matter what social fog or storm of partisan controversy his particular path may have to pass; he can also be assured that he will come out to his great satisfaction at some definite port of conclusion, no matter how often he has to alter his views or take fresh bearings on the way. It is no hardship to have to take a "new Negro" into account when one has to take stock of a "new world" anyway. It is because there is a new Europe, a new America, and a "new South" in fact, that there is a changed and changing Negro. Perhaps also this is the reason why the most hopeful and forward movement of the social mind on the race question is coming from youth reaching out in sympathy and understanding to the younger generation Negro. It pays to revise one's opinions about anything these days, but especially on a subject where the greatest obstacles to social peace and goodwill are the obsolete superstitions and outworn stereotypes that on both sides still cloud our social thinking and warp our social reactions in race relations in America. But these cannot persist side by side with the enlightenment that must come when the Negro capitalizes himself at his best, and that best is widely known and appreciated.

Social Analysis and Discussion

BRAWLEY, BENJAMIN GRIFFITH: *Your Negro Neighbor.* New York: Macmillan, 1918.

Africa and the War. New York: Duffield & Co., 1918.

CLARK, JESSIE McDOUGAL: *New Day for the Colored Woman Worker.* New York, 1922.

DANIEL, W. A.: *The Education of Negro Ministers.* New York; Doran Co., 1925.

GARVEY, AMY J.: *The Philosophy and Opinions of Marcus Garvey.* New York: Universal Publishing Co., 1923. A record of radical Negro thought.

HAYNES, GEORGE E.: *The Trend of the Races.* New York, 1923. A program of inter-racial attack on the race problem.

HARRISON, HUBERT H.: *When Africa Awakes.* New York: Poro Press, 1920. A radical expression in terms of the race problem as a world problem.

KING, WILLIS: *The Negro in American Life.* New York: Methodist Book Concern, 1926. A group study manual for inter-racial work.

MILLER, KELLY: *Out of the House of Bondage.* Chicago: Neale & Co., 1914.

The Appeal to Conscience. New York: Macmillan, 1918.

The Everlasting Stain. Washington, D. C.: The Associated publishers, 1924. Polemic discussion of the issues from 1914 to date.

ROGERS, J. A.: *From Superman to Man.* New York: Lenox Publishing Co., 1917. A polemic on the notion of race superiority.

ROMAN, CHARLES V.: *American Civilization and the Negro.* Philadelphia: F. A. Davis Co., 1916.

Scott, Emmett J.: *Negro Migration and the War.* New York: Oxford Press, 1920.

Wesley, Charles.: *Negro Labor in the United States.* New York: The Vanguard Press, 1927. The first important study of the economic role of the Negro in America.

The Negro's Cultural Background

Blyden, W. E.: *African Life and Customs.* London: C. M. Phillips, 1908. A scholarly vindication of African folk-ways.

Dubois, W. E. Burghardt: *The Negro.* New York: Henry Holt & Co., 1915. The best general survey to date of the Negro's past history and contributions to human civilization.

The Answer of Africa in "What is Civilization?" New York: Duffield & Co., 1926. A comparison of African ideas of life with other ideals of culture.

Ellis, George W.: *Negro Culture in West Africa.* New York: Neale & Co., 1914. A study of the contemporary West African tribal life.

Jabavu, D. D. T.: *The Black Problem.* Lovedale Press, South Africa, 1920. A native African leader's analysis of the colonial situation.

Johnson, Samuel: *The History of the Yorubas,* from the Earliest Times to the Beginning of the British Protectorate. London: J. Routledge & Sons, 1921. The most complete African tribal history extant.

Molema, S. M.: *The Bantu, Past and Present.* Edinburgh: W. Green & Son, 1920. An exhaustive study of this African federation of Peoples.

Plaatje, Solomon J.: *Sechuna Proverbs,* with Literal Translations and their European Equivalents. London: Keegan, Paul & Trench, 1916.

Historical Studies

BRAWLEY, BENJAMIN G.: *A Short History of the American Negro.* New York: The Macmillan Co., 1919. A short practicable manual of Negro history in America.

A Social History of the American Negro. New York Macmillan, 1921. A valuable interpretative historical survey.

CROMWELL, JOHN W.: *The Negro in American History.* Washington, D. C.: The American Negro Academy, 1914.

PICKENS, WILLIAM: *The New Negro,* his Political, Civic and Mental Status. Chicago: Neale Pub. Co., 1916.

SCOTT, EMMETT J.: *The American Negro in the World War.* Privately printed, 1919.

STEWARD, T. J.: *The Haitian Revolution,* 1791-1804. New York: Thos. Crowell, 1914.

TAYLOR, A. A.: *The Negro During Reconstruction in South Carolina.* Washington: The Associated Publishers, 1926.

The Negro in the Reconstruction of Virginia. Washington, D. C.: The Associated Publishers, 1927.

Collections of Negro Poetry

CULLEN, COUNTEE (Editor): *Caroling Dusk.* New York: Harper & Brothers, 1927. An anthology of younger generation poetry.

JOHNSON, JAMES WELDON (Editor): *The Book of American Negro Poetry.* New York: Harcourt, Brace & Co., 1922. A comprehensive anthology of Negro poetry, with a valuable introduction on "Negro Creative Genius."

LOCKE, ALAIN (Editor): *Four Negro Poets*: Pamphlet Poets Series. New York: Simon & Schuster, 1927. A popular handbook of the most representative current Negro verse.

Negro Poets

BRAITHWAITE, WM. STANLEY: *The House of Falling Leaves*. Boston: Luce & Co., 1908.
Sandy Star and Other Poems. Boston: The Brimmer Co., 1928. The original poems of the well known poetry critic and editor of "The Anthologies of Magazine Verse."

CARMICHAEL, J. S.: *From the Heart of a Folk.* Boston: The Cornhill Co., 1918.

COTTER, JOSEPH S., JR.: *The Bank of Gideon and Other Poems.* Boston: The Cornhill Co., 1918.

CULLEN, COUNTEE: *Color.* New York: Harper & Brothers, 1925.
Copper Sun. New York: Harper & Brothers, 1927. The verse of a leading contemporary poet.

DUNBAR, PAUL LAURENCE: *The Collected Poems of Paul Laurence Dunbar.* New York: Dodd, Mead & Co., 1920.

JOHNSON, CHARLES BERTRAM: *Songs of My People.* Boston: The Cornhill Co., 1918.

JOHNSON, FENTON: *Visions of the Dusk.* New York: 1915.
Songs of the Soil. New York, 1916. The poetry of protest and radical expression.

JOHNSON, GEORGIA DOUGLAS: *The Heart of a Woman and Other Poems.* Boston: The Cornhill Co., 1918.
Bronze. Boston: The Brimmer Co., 1922. The leading Negro woman poet.

JOHNSON, JAMES WELDON: *Fifty Years and After and Other Poems.* Boston: The Cornhill Co., 1917.

God's Trombones. Seven Negro Sermons in Verse. New York: The Viking Press, 1927. The first, an important contribution of the middle period of Negro poetry, and the latter, one of the outstanding contributions of the recent school.

HILL, LESLIE PINCKNEY: *The Wings of Oppression.* Boston: The Cornhill Co., 1917.

Toussaint L'Ouverture, a Dramatic History in 5 Acts. Boston: Christopher Press, 1928.

HUGHES, LANGSTON: *The Weary Blues.* New York: Alfred Knopf, 1926.

Fine Clothes to the Jew. New York: Alfred Knopf, 1927. One of the most representative contemporary Negro poets, known especially for his folk interpretations.

LAVIAUX, LEON: *The Ebon Muse and Other Poems,* translated by J. M. O'Hara, Portland, Me., 1914. The most brilliant of contemporary foreign Negro poets.

McKAY, CLAUDE: Harlem *Shadows.* New York, Harcourt, Brace & Co., 1922. A representative present generation poet.

SHACKELFORD, WM. H.: *Crackling Bread and Other Poems.* Philadelphia, 1916. Late dialect poems.

Fiction and Belles Lettres

ASHBY, WM. M.: *Redder Blood,* a novel. Chicago: Neale & Co., 1916.

BRAITHWAITE, WM. STANLEY: *The Poetic Year.* Boston: Small, Maynard & Co. 1917.

The Annual Anthologies of Magazine Verse, 1913-1927. Boston: Small, Maynard & Co. 1913-1918. Boston:

The Brimmer Co., 1918-1927. Representing the most significant sustained literary contemporary contribution of any Negro man of letters.

BRAWLEY, BENJAMIN G.: *The Negro in Literature and Art.* New York: Duffield & Co., 1918.

CHESTNUTT, CHARLES W.: *The House Behind the Cedars.* Boston: Houghton Mifflin Co., 1900.

The Marrow of Tradition. Boston: Houghton Mifflin Co., 1901. The Re-construction, its problems and settings, pictured by the pioneer modern Negro novelist.

COTTER, JOSEPH S., SR.: *Negro Tales.* New York: Cosmopolitan Press, 1912.

DuBOIS, W. E. BURGHARDT: *The Souls of Black Folk.* Chicago: McClurg, 1898. A classic of intimate spiritual interpretation of the Negro.

The Quest of the Silver Fleece, a novel. Chicago: McClurg, 1911. A novel of the South and its epic—cotton.

Darkwater. New York: Harcourt, Brace & Co., 1920. Interpretations in the vein of "Souls of Black Folk." Boston: The Stratford Co., 1924.

The Gift of Black Folk. The Stratford Co., 1924. An account of the contribution of black folk to the making of America.

Black Princess. New York: Harcourt, Brace & Co., 1928. A problem novel of the "intellectual" class on an international background.

FAUSET, JESSIE R.: *There is Confusion.* New York: Boni & Liveright, 1924. A novel of the educated classes in a Philadelphia and New York setting.

GRIMKE, ANGELINA: *Rachel, A Drama.* Boston: The Cornhill Co., 1920.

Johnson, James Weldon: *The Autobiography of an Ex-Colored Man*. New York: Sherman, French Co. 1912. Reprinted in The Blue Jade Library, Alfred Knopf, New York, 1927. A record of a typical personal experience in the upper strata of Negro Life.

Larsen, Nella: *Quicksands*. New York: Alfred Knopf & Co., 1928. A life-history of a Negro woman of culture, also on the international background.

Locke, Alain (Editor): *The New Negro: An Interpretation*. New York: A. & C. Boni, 1925. A compendium of the contemporary cultural expression of the "New Negro."

Maran, Rene: *Batouala* (Prix Concourt Novel, 1921). New York: Thos. Seltzer, 1922.

Kongo, A Novel of African Life. New York: A. & C. Boni, 1928. African novels of the distinguished French Negro author, the former being the Goncourt prize novel of 1921.

McKay, Claude: *Home to Harlem*. New York: Harper & Bros., 1928. A novel of Negro "low life," told realistically.

Nelson, Alice Dunbar (Editor): *Masterpieces of Negro Eloquence*. New York, 1914.

Pickens, William: *The Vengeance of the Gods*, a novel. Philadelphia: A. M. E. Book Concern, 1922.

Toomer, Jean: *Cane*, a novel. New York: Boni & Liveright, 1923. A brilliant poetic rendition of the South and the Negro in modernistic vein.

Walrond, Eric: Tropic Death. Boni & Liveright, 1926. Stories of the Caribbean.

WHITE, WALTER: *Fire in the Flint.* New York: Alfred Knopf, 1924.

Flight. New York: Alfred Knopf, 1926. Human document novels of contemporary Negro life.

WOODSON, CARTER G. (Editor): *Negro Orators and Their Orations.* Washington: The Assoc. Publishers. An authoritative documentary record of Negro public thought and publicists. 1926.

Negro Biography

ALEXANDER, CHARLES: *Battles and Victories of Allen Allensworth.* New York: Sherman, French Co. 1914.

ANDREWS, WM. McCANTS: *John Merrick,* a Biographical Sketch. Durham, N. C.: Seamons Press, 1920. The biography of the pioneer modern Negro business man.

BRAGG, GEORGE: *Men of Maryland.* Baltimore, 1925. Notable early publicists, church and anti-slavery leaders.

BRAWLEY, BENJAMIN G.: *Women of Achievement.* Baptist Home Mission Soc. Press, Boston, 1919.

BROWN, HALLIE Q.: *Homespun Heroines.* Xenia, Ohio: Aldine Pub. Co., 1927. Biographies of noted Negro women.

BULLOCK, RALPH W.: *In Spite of Handicaps.* Y. W. C. A. Publication, New York, 1927.

CORROTHERS, J. D.: *In Spite of the Handicap,* an Autobiography. New York: Doran, 1916.

CRAWFORD, GEORGE W.: *Prince Hall and his Followers.* New York: Crisis Pub. Co., 1914. An account of the founder of Negro Masonry.

FAUSET, ARTHUR H.: *For Freedom.* Philadelphia: Franklin Pub. Co., 1927. A modern school biographical supplementary reader, reflecting the spirit of the younger Negro mind.

GREEN, JOHN P.: *Truth Stranger Than Fiction,* an Autobiography. Cleveland, Ohio: Riehl Printing Co., 1920.

HAYNES, ELIZABETH R.: *Unsung Heroes.* New York: DuBois & Dill, 1921. A book of race biographies for children.

HUNTON, ADDIE W.: *Two Colored Women with the American Expeditionary Forces.* Brooklyn, N. Y.: Brooklyn Eagle Press, 1920.

JABAVU, D. D. T.: *The Life of John Tengo Jabavu.* Lovedale Press, South Africa, 1922.

JONES, LAURENCE C.: *Piney Woods and Its Story.* New York: Fleming H. Revells, 1922. The story of a backwoods school.

MASON, MONROE: *The American Negro Soldier with the Red Hand in France.* Boston: The Cornhill Co., 1920.

MOTON, ROBERT RUSSA: *Finding a Way Out, an Autobiography.* New York: Doubleday, Page & Co., 1920. The autobiography of the present head of Tuskegee Institute.

PICKENS, WILLIAM: *The Heir of Slaves.* New York, 1911. *Bursting Bonds.* Boston, 1923. An autobiography and a sequel, in which a college-bred Negro looks at life.

SCOTT, EMMETT J. and L. B. STOWE: *Booker T. Washington, Builder of a Civilization.* New York: Doubleday, Page & Co., 1916. The official biography of the founder of Tuskegee.

WALTERS, BISHOP ALEXANDER: *My Life and Work.* Chicago: Fleming H. Revell Co., 1917. A life story involving sidelights on the Niagara movement, and the Negro in politics in 1912-14.

WASHINGTON, BOOKER T.: Up *from Slavery*, an Autobiography. New York: Doubleday, Page & Co., 1901. The classic story of Booker T. Washington's own career.

WORK, MONROE N.: *The Negro Year Book.* Tuskegee: Tuskegee Division of Records, 1917-1927. An annual compendium of facts about the Negro.

Negro Music

BALLANTA, C. J. S.: *St. Helena Spirituals.* New York: Schirmer, 1925.

BROWN, LAWRENCE: *Five Spirituals.* London: Schott & Co., 1924.
Five Spirituals in the First Book of American Negro Spirituals. Viking Press, 1925.

BURLEIGH, HARRY T.: *Spirituals Arranged.* New York: Recordi, 1917-1926. Seculars.

DETT, NATHANIEL J.: *Negro Spirituals,* 3 Volumes. New York: John Church Co., 1919.
Religious Folk Songs of the Negro. Hampton Institute Press, 1927.

DITON, CARL R.: *Four Spirituals.* New York: Schirmer, 1912.
Four Negro Spirituals. New York: Schirmer, 1914.

HARE, MAUD CUNEY: *Six Creole Folk Songs.* New York: Fisher, 1921.

HANDY, W. C. and A. B. NILES: *Blues: an Anthology of Jazz.* New York: A. & C. Boni, 1926.

JOHNSON, JAMES WELDON & J. ROSAMOND JOHNSON: *The Book of American Negro Spirituals.* New York: The Viking Press, 1925.
The Second Book of American Negro Spirituals. New York: The Viking Press, 1926.

Talley, T. W.: *Negro Folk Rhymes.* New York: The Macmillan Co., 1922.

Cabin Memories, Four Spirituals. New York: Fisher, 1921.

White, Clarence Cameron: *Negro Folk Melodies.* Philadelphia: Presser & Co., 1927.

Work, John Wesley: *Folk Songs of the American Negro.* Nashville, Tenn.: Fisk University Press, 1915.

Magazines

The Crisis. Published by the National Association for the Advancement of Colored People, 69 Fifth Avenue, New York City, W. E. Burghardt DuBois, Editor. The pioneer journal of the intellectual school, with a program of investigation and publicity. Also devoted to encouraging literary and artistic expression among Negroes.

The Messenger. Published monthly at 2311 Seventh Avenue, New York City, A. Philip Randolph, Editor. A Journal that began as an expression of Negro radicalism, but has shifted from the strict economic radicalism to a program of independent criticism and reportorial features.

Opportunity. Published monthly since 1920 by the National Urban League, 17 Madison Avenue, New York City, Charles S. Johnson, Editor. A Journal promoting the program of urban social investigation and social work of the League and also the self expression program of the younger Negro school of thought.

The Journal of Negro History. Published quarterly by the Association for the Study of Negro Life and History, 1538 9th Street Washington, D. C., Carter G. Woodson, Editor. A scholarly research journal in Negro history and cultural origins.

The Southern Workman. Published monthly at Hampton Institute, Hampton, Va. A journal representing the Southern educational field and other activities.

The Home Mission College Review. Edited by Benjamin W. Brawley, Shaw University, Raleigh, N. C. Mainly devoted to the work of the colleges.

The Bulletin. Edited by C. J. Calloway, Tuskegee Institute, Ala. Organ of the National Association of Teachers in Colored Schools.

Occasional Papers Published by the Trustees of the John F. Slater Fund

1. Documents Relating to the Origin and Work of the Slater Trustees, 1894.
2. A Brief Memoir of the Life of John F. Slater, by Rev. S. H. Howe, D.D., 1894.
3. Education of the Negroes Since 1860, by J. L. M. Curry, LL.D., 1894.
4. Statistics of the Negroes in the United States, by Henry Gannett, of the United States Geological Survey, 1894.
5. Difficulties, Complications, and Limitations Connected with the Education of the Negro, by J. L. M. Curry, LL. D., 1895.
6. Occupations of the Negroes, by Henry Gannett, of the United States Geological Survey, 1895.
7. The Negroes and the Atlanta Exposition, by Alice M. Bacon, of the Hampton Normal and Industrial Institute, Virginia, 1896.
8. Report of the Fifth Tuskegee Negro Conference, by John Quincy Johnson, 1896.
9. A Report Concerning the Colored Women of the South, by Mrs. E. C. Hobson and Mrs. C. E. Hopkins, 1896.
10. A Study in Black and White, by Daniel C. Gilman, 1897.
11. The South and the Negro, by Bishop Charles B. Galloway, of the Methodist Episcopal Church, South, 1904.
12. Report of the Society of the Southern Industrial Classes, Norfolk, Va., 1907.
° 13. Report on Negro Universities in the South, by W. T. B. Williams, 1913.
c 14. County Teacher Training Schools for Negroes, 1913.
15. Duplication of Schools for Negro Youths, by W. T. B. Williams, 1914.
᾿ 16. Sketch of Bishop Atticus G. Haygood, by Rev. G. B. Winton, D.D., 1915.
17. Memorial Addresses in Honor of Dr. Booker T. Washington, 1916.
18. Suggested Course for County Training Schools, 1917.
19. Southern Women and Racial Adjustments, by Mrs. L. H. Hammond, 1917; 2nd ed., 1920.
20. Reference List of Southern Colored Schools, 1918; 2nd ed., 1921; 3d ed., 1925.
° 21. Report on Negro Universities and Colleges, by W. T. B. Williams, 1922.
22. Early Effort for Industrial Education, by Benjamin Brawley, 1923.
23. Study of County Training Schools, by Leo M. Favrot, 1923.
24. Five Letters of University Commission, 1927.
25. Native African Races and Culture, by James Weldon Johnson, 1927.
26. A Decade of Negro Self-Expression, by Alain Locke, 1928.